WHAT A

Beautiful

DECK!

A Step-By-Step Guide to Writing Highly Effective Business Presentations

Mason Argiropoulos

Lulu Publishing Services rev. date: 04/07/2019

Table of Contents

Chapter

INTRODUCTION

> According to most studies, people's number one fear
> is public speaking. Number two is death. This means
> to the average person, if you go to a funeral, you're
> better off in the casket than doing the eulogy.
> —Jerry Seinfeld

It's an otherwise routine Tuesday at the office when your boss stops by your desk unexpectedly. "You know that important project you've been working on? The VP just called me and not only wants a status update, but she wants our recommendation on how we should roll it out to the entire department. I'm going to need you to put together a presentation."

Regardless of your outward response to your boss, your inward response invariably sounds something like: "*Noooooooooooo!*" or "@#&$%" or similar. On top of the extra work that was just shoveled onto your already full plate, it was a heaping spoonful of your least favorite, nausea-inducing kind of work: writing a presentation.

The mere thought of this dastardly assignment brings your stress level to DEFCON 2. Presentation writing sucks. It's really hard. You never know how to start and can't possibly tell when the end product is ready for prime time. And, oh, by the way, you are never given enough time to muscle through the pain and deliver your best work.

For whatever reason, communication in the corporate world has a heavy reliance on this format. It is popular among requestors (i.e., clients, and those in your company higher up on the org chart than you) because the message and content are easier to digest when someone else molds it into the form of a story. It is a highly unpopular format for writers (i.e., you, if not already obvious) because you have to build the story, assemble the data and necessary information, make it look pretty, and on most occasions, wrestle with a projector or a web-sharing platform while your client or superiors await the upcoming entertainment. Why couldn't the request have been a concise email that drives straight to the punch line?

Okay, okay, let me suspend the conjuring of flashbacks from the ghosts of presentations past and press on to the brighter future. At the risk of sounding like a cliché, the truth is that this painful side effect doesn't have to automatically convey with corporate life. There is a means to take control of these situations and develop the skills to artfully construct stellar presentations without the writer's block, formatting hell, and other undesirables that come along for the ride in the current state.

In this short book, I will share a step-by-step process for how to organize your thoughts into an easy-to-follow story that is tailored to your audience while deftly avoiding other frequently-encountered presentation pitfalls that can dilute your message and/or damage your work. We will walk through preparation techniques to help you deliver your best and discuss other in-game adjustments you may need to make to react in real time. And we'll do our level best to have a little fun along the way.

Chapter **2**

THINGS NOT TO DO

Let's go back to our frightful situation from chapter 1: the highly distasteful request mandate has crash-landed on your desk, and since your past presentation disasterpieces have taken a long time, you want to get moving ASAP. You start looking for an old presentation template, save a new version of it with an appropriate name, begin looking for other slide pages that you can reuse …

Stop!

Over the years, I've observed many colleagues who take strange and misguided immediate first steps after being asked to write a presentation. I was a victim of this very same trap early in my career as well. I promise to quickly pivot to the aforementioned step-by-step process as advertised, but some of you may be reading this book and working on your presentation on the fly, and I therefore want to provide a virtual shock collar to halt some well-known bad behaviors of presentation writing. Without further ado:

False Start #1: Jumping into Microsoft PowerPoint and start building slides. This is akin to drilling Number 2 screws into random holes in your IKEA nightstand before you've read the directions. How do you know what slides are needed until you have a plan? As you will soon discover, selecting and entering input into your medium (e.g., PowerPoint, Keynote, Prezi, etc.) is not even "a thing" until chapter 5.

False Start #2: Retrieving past presentations to harvest slides and/or information. I don't have a DIY home project analogy for this, and it could be labelled False Start #1b, but the temptation to start cranking out the finished product is so alluring that the message bears repeating: do not open your presentation app because you are not ready.

False Start #3: Creating graphs and charts that you want to use in your presentation. Okay, so you didn't open your presentation program (nice display of self-control!) but this is an inefficient use of your energy as well. How can you know what data to show if you haven't yet developed a hypothesis or a recommendation?

As in my IKEA analogy, if you are reading this guide step by step while working on your presentation, this section could simply be labeled: "Don't Do Anything Just Yet and Please Continue Reading." Great. Now on to chapter 3.

Chapter **3**

UNDERSTAND THE REQUEST

Having navigated the false start pitfalls, we can now transition from what not to do to some real actions we can do.

Let's go back to the moment when your boss or client dropped the bombshell, giving birth to the presentation request. Before you let her leave, there are a few really important pieces of information you should extract (if the answers are known) in order to properly prepare for battle.

Who is my audience? Is it just the department VP, or will there be other people there who may not know much about the project in the first place?

What is the purpose of the presentation? Is it just an update? Am I asking for more resources or time? Are we ready to ask for approval for our recommendation on rollout?

When is the presentation due? Do you (my manager) need to see it ahead of time? Is there a specific deadline or meeting that is already scheduled?

Where is the presentation going to be delivered? In person or over the phone? Or perhaps over video? If in person, will we be in the

VP's office or in the cavernous conference room on the third floor with the ancient and finicky overhead projector?

How should my presentation be delivered? Can I use Keynote or does it have to be in MS PowerPoint? Does it need to be in pdf form so she can easily read it on her tablet? Or does anyone care what program I use?

Your manager may not know the answers to all of these questions, and you may notice her growing tired of your inquisition before you tick every box. Don't sweat it in the moment—or panic if you are reading this after-the-fact and missed the chance to ask at the time the assignment was given—but you will need to find out the answers to these questions before too long. If time and/or patience is running short, focus on the first three (who, what, and when) since those will be the most critical pieces of input for you to get started. Where and how can be determined at a later date.

Note that I omitted *why* from the list. Not because it wouldn't be insightful to understand the reason behind the request (e.g., concern about slow progress, extreme interest in your project, desire to create work for you, etc.) but I'm sure you've found that responding to a request from your superiors with a *why* question is not always wise. I often respond to similar questions from my kids, neither of whom have the optional Tact Filter feature, with the "because Daddy asked you to do it" reason. Your boss may give you a similar retort.

Chapter 4

WRITING DOWN THE NARRATIVE

Of all the menacing aspects of writing a presentation, perhaps the most difficult is the act of getting started. You are in all likelihood familiar with the term *writer's block*, a condition used to describe the challenge authors face when they don't know how to articulate a particular part of their novel or simply aren't sure what they want to write. This happens to presentation writers too, and in my experience, it occurs most often at the very outset of the assignment. You have the deep desire to write a Pulitzer Prize-contending presentation but can't figure out how to craft the first sentence.

Unless you skipped ahead to this section, you are by now aware that the exact place not to begin is by finding or making slides in PowerPoint or your other vehicle of choice. The best first step in any presentation, assuming you have already at least identified your *who*, *what*, and *when*, is to construct your narrative.

That's great, but what's a narrative? Other than doubling as a fancy word your English lit professor may have thrown around on occasion, it is simply an outline of a story or presentation in sentence form. If done properly, you could simply read your narrative aloud in thirty to sixty seconds and, in doing so, have covered the entire story from context to punch line at a high level.

It serves as the backbone of your presentation, and all of the other supporting information, data, and details form the rib cage that hangs from it.

The best way to illustrate the concept of a narrative is through an example. Let's pretend that we are writing a presentation that summarizes the movie *Ferris Bueller's Day Off*, which hopefully you have either (a) watched a baker's dozen times at a minimum like yours truly, or (b) by this point in your life, determined that you have no interest in seeing it but can still follow the example narrative to aid with your own presentation building.

Ferris Bueller, a high school student, decides that he wants to take a day off from school and parade around the greater Chicago metro area.

To enable this, he hatches an elaborate plan to fake an illness in order to convince his parents that he should stay home in bed while they go to work.

He rigs up a body double to fool his parents into thinking he is in bed when they check on him.

Meanwhile, he bounces from activity to activity around town, including such antics as getting his girlfriend and best friend excused from school and going to a ballgame at Wrigley Field.

His school principal is convinced that Ferris is pulling a fast one and goes to great lengths to catch him in the act.

This pursuit culminates in a frantic race for Ferris to get home in time to get back into his room before his parents return home and/or the principal catches him.

Ferris ultimately gets home in time, the principal gets attacked by a dog, and no one is the wiser about Ferris Bueller's adventures while "at home sick."

There you have it; the hard part of your presentation is actually done. In seven full-sentence bullet points, I summarized the plot of a two-hour movie. Sure, there are a lot of entertaining details I left out, but the basic nuts and bolts are captured, and other than perhaps some more minor side plots, any additional color that would be added to the movie builds on one of these seven points.

You may be thinking that summarizing the script of a well-known story is much easier than writing the actual script from scratch. That may be true, but chances are that if you are being asked to write the presentation, no one in your company or organization is more capable than you at telling your story. Each story is unique, just like the one you are being asked to write, but there are some common components of most business-oriented narratives that can be used as a guide. Let's begin by determining which type of presentation you are about to give.

Type #1: The Recommendation

The most common type of presentation in my experience is one I refer to as the recommendation. This is a situation where you, as the project leader, salesperson, analyst, or some other role in which you have a fair amount of expertise in whatever you are doing, are asked to recommend a solution or action to someone who is empowered to make decisions on your recommendations. In these instances, the decision-maker is often a department head, senior executive, or another individual higher up in your organization, or if in a client/vendor relationship, at the risk of stating the obvious, it is likely that you are the vendor, salesperson, or service provider, and your audience is the client.

While there may be a temptation to immediately "cut to the chase," the best approach is generally to build up to your recommendation by telling a story, in the same manner that best-selling books and award-winning movies contain an interesting plot that builds to a climax. It makes for good entertainment, and you want your audience to be interested in the material you are presenting instead of checking their email, social media accounts, stock portfolios, or the myriad of other potential distractions on their phones.

Don't be intimidated. Most recommendations follow a pretty standard sequence:

Situation: Even though personal torture may come to mind, there is always some form of business reason that prompted whatever it is that you are working on that must now be spun into a beautiful spiderweb of a presentation. If it is a project of some kind, then there must be some purpose to the project, which might range from saving the company money, increasing revenue, minimizing risk, or improving customer experience, to name a few. It is important to ground your audience with the business situation that forms the basis of your recommendation, even at the risk of sounding obvious. This can often be done with one or two bullets in your narrative, but these short statements are highly necessary in constructing the foundation of your story.

Complication: There is almost always a reason why the recommendation you are building toward isn't easy and straightforward. This is because there is some complicating factor, hurdle, issue, challenge, roadblock, or other analogy to convey that "something is making this harder." If the situation was super simple, like "the office dog is thirsty" and water is easily accessible, then not only is there no real complication, but it also means that you don't need to write a presentation to convince your superiors that you recommend hooking up the pooch with some *agua*. In other words, this complication is an important piece of data that your audience needs to understand so they don't undermine your presentation by jumping to an uninformed conclusion.

Analysis: Once you have laid out the basic background and challenges, you will want to spend an appropriate amount of time explaining your approach and rationale, ideally with supporting data, so that your recommendation has some basis behind it. When I say "appropriate," I mean that you need to find the right balance between giving your audience a concise logical foundation to support your recommendation and sufficient data/backup/analysis without plunging too deep into minute detail. This is where you need to consider several factors such as the time allotted for your presentation and the detail-orientation (or lack thereof) of the key decision-makers in your audience panel.

Solution recommendation: Alas, you have now arrived at the highlight of your story, where you have fully piqued the interest of your audience and can pull back the curtain that hides your prized recommendation. There has obviously been a significant amount of background, data, and analysis to support your noble suggestion, and if the prior sections of your presentation have been well thought out and communicated, the recommendation should be one that the majority of the room would have also put forth if they were in your shoes. So here you need to ensure that your recommendation doesn't appear to come out of nowhere, and it must also be specific and action-oriented. If you simply recommend that the team "work harder," do not anticipate a warm reception from your audience.

Contingent action: A strong recommendation presentation always concludes with a specific and tangible set of next steps, contingent upon the recommendation being approved. Your audience will want to know that you have thought through the answer to the "okay, so now what do we do?" question that in some form immediately follows a successful acceptance of your proposal.

This can often be a simple one-page list of actions, owners, and projected due dates to serve as a high-level guide for how your recommendation becomes a reality. If they don't automatically volunteer it, you should ask your audience for feedback on these steps since they often either manage the individual assignees of your tasks or perhaps have strong opinions about when the actions should be taken (spoiler alert: they usually will want you to get things done faster than you propose unless your due dates are clearly too optimistic).

Here is an example of a made-up recommendation:

- Everyone is aware that we have been struggling to keep up with the volume of inbound calls to our call center.
- This problem is about to get worse because our peak call volume season starts next month, and my best recruiter just quit.
- To add staff quickly, I analyzed two options: (1) partner with an external recruiting firm, and (2) partner with a temporary staffing agency.
- The recruiting firm charges a fixed rate per hire with a guarantee while the staffing firm provides a stream of people with a 25 percent markup on the hourly wages.
- Since we have limited funding, we ran some cost analysis to see which is the most cost-effective given our typical turnover rate.
- Even though it will take them slightly longer to provide people, the recruiting firm should be 15 percent less expensive while providing the same quality of employee.
- Since we expect volumes to stay high, we will likely want to keep as many of the placed hires as we can.
- I am therefore recommending that we partner with Acme Recruiting Firm due to its cost effectiveness, past history with us, and strong recent references from other clients.
- Assuming we move forward, I will need to have their contract renewed by Legal, a purchase order approved by Finance,

and a target date of two weeks from now to have their first placements in training.

Type #2: The Update

If you are asked to provide an update on your project, process, operation, results, or any other aspect of what you do, to maximize your likelihood of wowing the audience, it would still behoove you to build it into a story instead of a series of update slides. One of the most common narrative structures for updates follows the background, accomplishments, status, issues, next steps, and assistance model. Here is what each of these means:

Background: Every update narrative should start with a minimum of one statement (occasionally two) that sets background and context for the presentation. No audience member appreciates the discussion starting in the middle of the story, just as most people are annoyed when they arrive twenty minutes late to a movie already in progress. The background statement usually provides context for the purpose of the meeting, an overview of the project or process that sets the stage for the forthcoming update, or a short recap of the initial problem that needs to be solved.

Accomplishments: Unless your update is that you haven't actually done anything on your project (in which case you will likely have a very short meeting and an extremely underwhelmed audience), chances are that you and your team have actually gotten something done. Since you have been able to eloquently communicate the status of your project through the prior section of your presentation, at this juncture you can now describe the specifics that are in the rearview mirror. This is important for a few reasons: (1) it connects your audience to tangible actions within your project to build understanding; (2) it is important in bridging to the other sections of your presentation, as you will see; and (3) it gives you a dose of credibility to convey that you are not 100 percent talk and 0 percent action.

Two cautionary warnings to heed when listing the project's accomplishments are: (a) maintain an appropriate length and level of detail, and (b) keep the bragging and selling to a minimum. You have to consider your audience carefully here since there will be a temptation to provide the longest list of completed actions possible and talk about how great you and your team are doing. In most cases, you will be best served by hitting the highlights instead of the exhaustive inventory, and it's always best to stay objective when articulating what you've done and what you perhaps have not done. Your audience will become highly skeptical if they feel they are being sold to.

Status: Once you have provided your background and accomplishments on this effort, their next question will undoubtedly be some form of "Where are we?" To proactively address this query, the next part of your narrative should be a high-level update on where things stand—quite simply, the status of your project. Many companies and organizations dig the three-option "stoplight" framework, which, if you are unfamiliar, operates as follows:

- Green = on track, with minimal to no issues
- Yellow = on track but unsure if the project will stay on track due to more significant issues or foreseen roadblocks that could impede progress
- Red = currently running behind the timeline and/or over budget and likely with significant outstanding issues

In your narrative, you will want to include a single sentence that sums up how your project is doing against its plan, and selecting one of the colors above is often an easy way to convey the status of it.

Issues: Except for those rare situations where everything is running so swimmingly smooth, your project has at least one if not several issues that are derailing (or have the potential to derail) the effort. This is a good time in the narrative to summarize those current and/or future roadblocks. Sharing your top issues or concerns with your audience will demonstrate that you are aware of the risks and challenges that you are facing. Not addressing issues or potential issues is likely to be a red flag for your audience, who may think that you are either trying to tell them only the good parts of the story or that you don't have a handle on the hurdles that could slow you down.

Next steps: Unless the heart of your update is that your project is finished, then you have more work still ahead of you, and your audience will be curious as to your next few moves. As such, your next steps should be summarized in your narrative. While these will be highly customized to your specific project at hand, your next steps are frequently comprised of either delivering on your next few milestones or resolving your most pressing issues. In either case, your audience is interested in action, and if a future update presentation is in the cards, they will want to know what you plan to include in your list of accomplishments the next time you are in front of them.

Assistance: Some update narratives can actually end with the summary of next steps, but there are times when you may need something from your audience to keep your project on track. I like to call this "assistance," and the end of your presentation is often the best time to ask for any help that you may need from one or more of your audience members. By positioning this at the very end, you will have given your audience the full download on your project, and at this juncture they would have the most context to understand the feasibility and appropriateness of your request. If applicable to your storyline, a simple sentence asking for the help you need would be the perfect way to close your update narrative.

Here is an example for a fictitious project status update:

- As you know, we began Project ABC two months ago to better understand why so many of our widgets are being returned with claims that they don't function properly.
- Overall, the analysis phase of the project is on track.
- At this point, we have surveyed over two hundred customers and determined that over 80 percent of the defects fall into three categories.
- The biggest issue we have uncovered is that one of the defects involves an overheated battery, which could lead to a product recall.
- The key next steps are for us to meet with the manufacturer and our battery supplier to better understand each of these three primary defect types.
- Based on what we are seeing, we are going to ask for your help in securing product safety resources to assist with the battery issue at a minimum.

Type #3: The Discussion

Occasionally requests are made for presentations that are neither quite a recommendation nor a simple update. In these cases, the call to order is for a discussion, debate, or decision where a group needs to convene to talk through two or more options on how to proceed and where no clear recommendation can be made.

The format of discussion presentations tends to vary a bit more than their more straightforward peers, but all discussion decks culminate in the teeing up of a dialogue among the audience members once the background, pros and cons, and other pertinent information has been covered. If there is a standard flow for the discussion, it would go something like this:

Situation/complication/analysis: If there is a need to discuss a complicated issue that does not have a clear recommendation, then the appropriate background and detail need to kick off your presentation to build toward the climactic dialogue that will ensue later in the show. In other words, your discussion presentation will start off in the same flow as the recommendation type by first summarizing the situation you find yourself in, the complication that is making life hard, and the analysis you performed to date that brings the picture into focus and foreshadows the potential options that will be presented. From here, the discussion format diverges because no single solution recommendation is being presented.

Summary of options: Without a straightforward solution to recommend, the next step in the discussion type of presentation is to lay out the range of options that are being considered to address the problem or opportunity. This could be a binary exercise where there are only two paths at the fork in the road, or there could be several legitimate options from which a winner could be chosen. It is important to demonstrate to your audience that while you aren't in a position to recommend a solution, you aren't simply presenting a problem and dumping it into their laps to address. You must think through whatever credible options that you can in order to have a constructive conversation with your audience that maximizes the odds of arriving at a decision before the room clears out.

Pros and cons: To take the preparation one step further, once your options are revealed, it is wise to accompany them with some thoughtful pluses and minuses, often referred to as pros and cons. If one of your choices has all pros and no cons, guess what: you are writing a recommendation presentation and need to rewind a few pages in this book. Said differently, all of your options should have some mix of advantages and disadvantages, and here is where you will be relying on your audience to determine which factors are the most important. Cost versus speed. Predictability versus profitability. The combinations aren't quite endless, but there are many out there, and if you have the right folks around the table, the collective mindshare should be able to help you sift through all of it.

Other factors: This section is optional and may or may not be needed, but if there are additional considerations or constraints that need to be understood prior to the discussion commencing, this would be the place to do it. Examples could include an important deadline for when the decision needs to be made or downstream implications of the options chosen on other departments, vendors, etc. The important point here is that you want to put as much information on the table as you can to help your audience make the most informed decision possible. You would hate to be sent packing to pull more detail together and deal with the administrative hassle of finding a future date and time when everyone is available.

Contingent action(s): Like the recommendation format, there is a section on contingent actions, but in this case they cover your range of options. For example, if we proceed down Path #1, these four actions will need to be completed. Depending on how hungry your audience is for that climactic dialogue we keep mentioning, this section could come before the discussion if its details are relevant to the decision-making process, or it can serve as the wrap-up to the discussion where you zero in on the contingent actions specific to the path chosen. Either way, it is important to have thought through the next steps as best you can for all options so that you can leave the meeting with a mutual understanding of the next several tasks once a decision is made.

Here is a sample discussion narrative:

- As you know, our $250M downtown luxury condo complex is running behind schedule by three months.

- To complicate our situation, the project is also running over budget by $20M.
- Since we can't let the project timeline slip any further, we need to either reduce the scope of the project or secure additional funding.
- We have analyzed a variety of options, but only three of them have any real credibility.
- Option #1: we can take out an additional loan (second lien).
- Option #2: we can downgrade the condo fixtures from ultra-high-end luxury to a more modest but high-quality variety.
- Option #3: we can reconfigure the roof to remove the pool, solar panel array, and helipad.
- Option #1 allows us to maintain our original scope and promise to those customers who put down a deposit on units; the disadvantage would be that the debt comes with a very high interest rate and lengthens our payback period by nine months.
- Option #2 avoids the additional debt and still keeps the scope of the building amenities, but we would need to redo our marketing materials and somehow explain the changes to the early depositors.
- Option #3 keeps the condo fixtures in the original design and avoids extra debt, but we would have just one pool and more expensive utilities, and we would have to explain the amenity changes to our depositors and future buyers of the units.
- We need to make a decision before the end of next week since I need to place orders for countertops, kitchen and bathroom fixtures, and we are set to begin reinforcing the roof infrastructure early next month.
- I have the marketing team prewired and ready to change materials and update existing customers if needed, and I've sourced three lenders for the additional financing if we go down that path instead.

- Let's talk through the options and see if we can make a decision today, or if not, what information or data is needed to make a decision within the next seven days.

The best part about the narrative exercise is that it can be done in any format or medium, handwritten or electronic. Remember, your presentation application should still be closed at this point. I have written presentation narratives on a blank sheet of printer paper, in Microsoft Word, in an empty email draft, using Evernote, on a whiteboard, on the back of a page of a page-a-day calendar, and several other random locations. The point is that the hard work is in the thought process of constructing your story, and it should therefore be performed in whatever format is either the easiest or most comfortable for you at the time.

Bulletproofing the Narrative

At this point in your journey, you have successfully written a narrative outline for your presentation, and so it must be time to begin hammering out slides, right? Not quite, although we are getting closer. Before you put those artistic powers to use, it is always a good idea to validate that your story hangs together. There are a variety of ways to do this, and your particular situation may drive you down a specific path, but here are a few ways to verify that you have a tight outline versus one with holes:

- Ask a friend or colleague to read through your narrative. These "outside eyes" may notice something you didn't or ask good questions to help you further prepare.
- See if your boss or one of your audience members could review it to see if you are on track. This is obviously situation-dependent and may not be an option given the individuals and personalities in question. As a manager, I have never turned down the request to review a presentation outline.

- Simply review it yourself if you haven't already. It is usually best to put a little distance in between the completion of the narrative and your bulletproofing review to allow for a potentially different perspective. In other words, sleep on it, do some other work or activity in between, or just take your mind off the presentation for at least a couple hours to allow for a fresh look.

While you may be itching to start building content, this step will save you time later in the process. What you are trying to avoid through the bulletproofing step is having to modify your narrative partway through your presentation crafting, which results in wasted effort and unnecessary rework.

Chapter 5

CHOOSE YOUR MEDIUM

No, I am not referring to the spiritual person who can explain your presentation content using telepathy or other ethereal channels. I'm talking about the software (or in very rare cases, physical "canvas") into which your presentation will be housed. This may already be set in stone based on standard office protocol, in which case if you are effectively being forced into using Microsoft PowerPoint, you can skip this section if you prefer. If your medium of choice is still in question, or if you are simply curious to know what else is out there beside the corporate-beloved PowerPoint, this chapter will walk through the lesser-known options.

Let me start though with the eight-hundred-pound gorilla in the presentation space—**Microsoft PowerPoint**. It is by far the world's most popular presentation package, which has been a core part of the Microsoft Office suite along with cousins Word and Excel since 1989.[1] It has seen several upgrades and changes over the years, but the basic premise is still the same: it helps organize your story in a series of individual slides (yes, as in slides from slideshow projection systems, first introduced in the 1930s) using lots of customizable text and drawing tools along with templates, animation, and many other functions to help you make your slides as pretty as can be. If

---

[1] Acquired podcast, www.acquired.fm, May 4, 2018, Season 2, Episode 7: PowerPoint.

for some reason you have never used PowerPoint, stop here and do two things: (1) go watch a YouTube or Udemy video on the basics of how to use it, and (2) email me since you will be the first adult I know who has never used it.

Google Slides. For any of you Gmail users, you have probably noticed that Google has created its own version of the Big Three, responding to Microsoft's Word, Excel, and PowerPoint with Docs, Sheets, and Slides respectively. These tools are all free and have a lot of the same features of their Microsoft counterparts despite holding a much lesser-known status. It is actually compatible with PowerPoint and is automatically available online or offline, so you have more flexibility in how to connect to your file to display it. Slides also has built-in templates that you can leverage if there isn't already a specific company-branded version that you are compelled to use.

Apple Keynote. Not to be outdone, our friends from Cupertino have their own software tool for presentations called Keynote. Like PowerPoint and Slides, it has a full range of features to handle any presentation writing needs, with perhaps a slightly easier-to-use interface compared to its PC-based counterpart especially for frequenters of other Apple applications. Keynote now has the ability to open PowerPoint slides (as many of the Microsoft competitors can) but PowerPoint does not reciprocate. As such, the use of Keynote comes with the same cautions as Slides regarding compatibility for sharing and presenting.

Prezi. If you aren't familiar with Prezi, it is an online SaaS tool that takes a different approach to constructing presentations. Prezi gives the user an infinite canvas on which to create content, and you then determine the path of your presentation by selecting various snapshots of different sections of your canvas in a specific sequence. The system automatically pans to the appropriate section and zooms in or zooms out to display the relevant snapshot on a full-screen view. Prezi has a number of fancy features, including a utility that allows you to import content directly from PowerPoint, providing the ability to then rearrange content into any flow path your heart desires. Accessing your Prezi presentation requires only an internet connection and can even be downloaded into a "show" if you have to run it from your local PC for some reason.

Other online. There are a variety of other online software tools for creating presentations. **FlowVella**, **Ludus**, and **Zoho Show** are just a few of those names. Each has some interesting features or specialties depending on how fancy or dynamic your presentation needs to be. Unless you have a lot of browsing time to find the very best platform among the many options available online, it is probably best to stick to the standard software that is most common within your company or client's organization.

Microsoft Excel. I have seen Excel (or other spreadsheet tools for that matter) work well in certain circumstances as a presentation medium, especially if your presentation involves heavy use of tabular data or any on-the-fly calculations. Instead of slides, you can simply create different tabs across the bottom of the spreadsheet and you can manually click through them to tell your story. While Excel has many of the same drawing features as PowerPoint, it is not built to display a clean-looking presentation and requires additional formatting to shape it into something that might resemble a more traditional PowerPoint deck. However, if your presentation involves variable models, adjusting calculations, or other on-the-fly data manipulation for effect or flexibility, Excel can be rigged to work as an effective presentation medium if the situation calls for it.

Analog. This would be the catch-all category for any handwritten presentation, most likely using an easel with large sheets of paper, a whiteboard, overhead transparency projector (if you can still find one) or any other physical medium devoid of the conveniences of software. I suppose there may be certain scenarios where this might play—Zach Galifianakis pulls it off well in one of his stand-up routines—but for the rest of us, it's best to stick to the electronic versions for obvious reasons. As you can see from all of the potential software avenues described above, any of them can work perfectly well as your medium for displaying supporting visuals while you tell your story.

Chapter 6

IT'S ALMOST CONSTRUCTION TIME! BUT NOT YET.

We are very close to slide building—really close—but please hang tight, fight the urge, and keep reading.

At this point in your journey, you have written a powerful narrative and made it even stronger with a heavy dose of bulletproofing. You have also chosen your medium. The next step in the process is to convert this into a presentation outline, which will serve as your blueprint for the slides you will need to construct.

I have found that the easiest way to execute this conversion is to take your narrative and organize it into slides/frames/pages/tabs, depending on which medium you have selected. I will generally make reference to slides since the odds favor PowerPoint as your chosen medium; the rest of you can sub in the appropriate name for each singular idea for the word slide as needed.

You will find that, in many cases, each one of the statements in your narrative can and should represent a single slide, and a default structure for your presentation could simply be to take each statement and put it at the top of its own individual slides. There are cases where statements are better organized into groups of as few as two and usually no more than five. The number and size of your groups will be somewhat dependent on how much time you are allotted for your presentation. As an example, if you have a rather long narrative but need to deliver a twenty-minute presentation, you will need to do some grouping to get your presentation down to fewer than ten slides.

How does one determine which statements are best grouped and which should stand alone? You may need to iterate on this a bit, but the answer is most often found in the supporting data, graphs, charts, pictures, diagrams or other visual aids you plan to use to support your story. In other words, if you have a graph that provides the backup to a single statement, then that combination will likely fill out one slide in your presentation. If you have a statement with no real backup data or supporting visual, and it is a statement that, while important, really works best when paired or grouped with other statements in your narrative, then you will want to design a slide that displays this cluster of statements without giving your audience a reading assignment. (In the next chapter, I will share some tips on how to avoid these outcomes.)

Once you have transposed your narrative into a collection of slides, it is now time for slide construction!

Chapter

7

FINALLY! CONSTRUCTION TIME! FOR REAL!

For those of you who heeded my advice to postpone all slide construction until I said go, congratulations on resisting the temptation up until this point. You made it, and we are now going to dive into some tips and techniques on turning your eloquent and bulletproofed narrative into a compelling page-turner.

For those of you who already started writing slides, thank you for at least skimming this section, and I hope that this chapter makes you realize how much time you wasted building content without following the proper order of operations.

With your freshly mapped presentation outline as your guide, go ahead and open your desired application so you can begin inputting content. To make the task a little less daunting, one approach you can take is to simply create a slide for each piece of your presentation outline and add comments in the middle of the page as self-instructions for what content ultimately needs to be added. Examples might be, "revenue by quarter graph," "project plan table," "test results chart," and so on. From there, you now just need to add your content in as easy to read and see format as your subject matter allows.

By now, you have worked so diligently to carefully craft your narrative and slide outlining, preparing for what will be a hugely compelling story for your audience. One surefire way to pull the rug out from under your story is to populate your slides with messy, poorly formatted, overly detailed, unclear, contradictory, and/or other negative-sounding adjectives to describe visual aids or supporting information that isn't as carefully constructed as your outline. The good news is that we aren't talking about brain surgery; the guidelines I will share should be common sense to most. Despite what are otherwise logical directions, some combination of bad habits, lack of attention to detail, or extremely misaligned audience reading must be to blame for the countless presentations I've seen whose eye-roll-inducing content would distract even the most focused critic from the core story.

With that in mind, please do yourself and your audience members a favor and heed these words of advice:

No Hail of Bullets

Bullet points are the Goldilocks of any presentation slide: they work well when used in moderation but using too few looks odd and too many overpowers the eyes much like Papa Bear's near-boiling porridge burns taste buds. Most often, people err on the side of displaying too much content rather than too little, and the result is a busy page with a font size that renders your presentation unreadable for the back of the room. Here are a few rules of thumb, coincidentally organized in bulleted form:

Cap the number of bullet points at five. Any more than this, and you are either providing too much detail or you need another slide to break it up (hint: it's likely the former).

Limit the length of the bullet point to no more than two lines of text. Any more words than this and your bullet point will more closely resemble a paragraph or short story.

Use the same sentence type and structure throughout. For example, if all of your bullets start with action verbs, please make sure they are in the same tense.

Note also that, while certain slides will best convey the main message if an appropriate set of three to five bullet points with text are used, do not take this approach on every slide. Page after page of bulleted text, while not painful in individual doses, will weaken the attention of your audience if used too frequently. In short, mix it up with data, graphs, tables, and even a picture if it fits in context.

Don't Give Your Audience an Eye Exam

A corollary to the bullet management guidance described in the previous section is the eye test rule. This rule states that you must not make your audience members squint or strain to read the text on your slide. More directly, make the font size large enough for every word on your slides such that it can be easily read in the back of the room by someone who doesn't necessarily have 20/20 vision.

Acceptable font sizes will vary by font type (e.g., Arial is a larger font than Times New Roman pound-for-pound), the size of the room, and the size of the projection surface, so sometimes twelve-point type is large enough, and sometimes it isn't. So while you will need to do a little testing to see if your slides can be read easily, you can deploy a few tactics to obviate this concern:

1. Adhere to the bullet rule. If you have five short statements or fewer on one page, you can keep increasing the text size until you run out of room on the page. Or if you are using Prezi, you

can zoom in close enough to have the text expand to cover the full screen.

2. Keep your noncontent space in the minority. I would use the term whitespace here, but not every slide background is white (even if that is the default in PowerPoint). The point here is to not let your text, charts, and occasional graphics drown in your slide background sea; use the entire page and zoom or increase the size of these objects to sufficiently dominate the page. After all, this is what your audience came to see, not your fancy wallpaper.

3. Don't overcomplicate your pages. Unless your presentation is meant to be read as a stand-alone document without the accompaniment of your color commentary, don't feel compelled to include every comment, detail, and piece of data on the page. Your slides should contain the main points and highlights, which you can then embellish as talking points during your show. If you include all of your embellishments on the page, not only will it be hard to digest for your audience, but you will also appear to be simply regurgitating the presentation contents as opposed to sharing accretive commentary. Give your audience a reason to listen to you while they read what you've produced.

Silly Rabbit, Clip Art Is for Kids

When I say "even a picture if it fits in context," the more direct message here is "use pictures cautiously and sparingly." You may be asking how this is possible when a picture is worth a thousand words. That may be true in certain circumstances, but it is extremely difficult to find a picture that is going to be *the* precise visual aid you need to help your audience digest the message you are trying to convey. Not to say that it is impossible; the right photograph or stock graphic can add interest and color to your story, and its association can help your audience better remember what you have described. However, more often than not, the picture or graphic is a useless space-filler that (a) cheapens your presentation, and (b) urges you to follow this pattern on other slides, turning your presentation into a photo album or a cartoon reel.

That said, visual aids can be very powerful when used correctly, so please don't take from this chapter that all photos and graphics are banned from use. It is completely fine—and helpful—to include them in the right circumstances, but most of the time if you are searching for the right complementary visual aids, a graph or table should be the more frequently used utensil in the drawer.

Avoiding Gaffes with Graphs

There is perhaps no better way to display data than using graphs and charts. These tools visualize what would otherwise be a table of numbers, allowing the human eye to see patterns and relationships in a clear manner. A variety of flavors are available, and not only is it important to choose the right one, but you also must format it correctly to maximize its information-conveying power with your audience. I lost count many years ago of the number of improperly selected and poorly formatted graphs to which I have been subjected, but the guide below will help you avoid similar embarrassment.

Let's start by choosing the right graph or chart. I'll go through the most commonly used among the standard options available in the Microsoft Office suite as a starting point. Over the years, our friends at Microsoft have added additional graph formats with more advanced uses that are less commonly needed, so if none of the types I describe fit the bill, a bit of offline homework can uncover the right one among the other available choices. If you are using a presentation medium other than PowerPoint or Excel, the graph templates may have slightly different names, but it shouldn't be hard to locate the appropriate analog.

Column/bar chart: One of the most commonly used graph formats is the column (vertical)/bar (horizontal) chart. These graphs are used to show varying quantities against different categories, such as the number of units sold by month or the average price of different products. In my experience, column charts are more common than their horizontal cousin since we tend to think of amplitude as something that goes up and down as opposed to left to right, but both can be used for the same function.

The column or bar chart format is best used when you have somewhere between two and ten categories that are (a) distinct from one another and/or, (b) equidistant from each other. If you have more than ten categories, you will more likely want to use a line graph, and if your categories are numbers that are not equidistant from one another, an XY scatter plot is the better weapon of choice. Both of these chart types are described in subsequent sections.

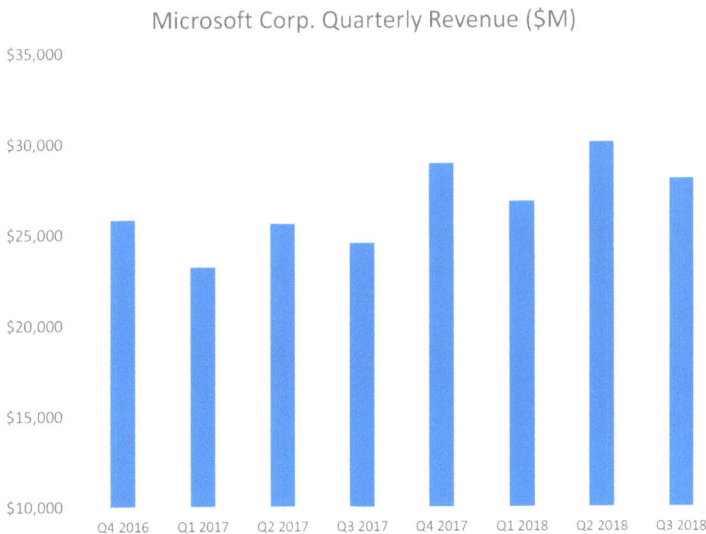

Microsoft Corp. Quarterly Revenue ($M)

Two variations of the column/bar charts worth noting are the **stacked column** and the **waterfall**. The stacked column (or bar) allows you to show the cumulative totals of multiple components within a category, such as the percentage of sales from three different products by quarter for several quarters. The waterfall chart takes a starting point and ending point on a column chart and shows incremental up and down steps to bridge from the first data point to the last. These are best used to graphically represent variance analyses, such as the puts and takes between a quarterly budget and the actual result.

Line graph: Another commonly leveraged format is the line graph, which works very similarly to the column chart in that it displays quantities across a range of categories. Line graphs tend to work best where the categories are on the X axis, and the quantities are on the Y axis, but since the output is displayed as either a series of dots or a series of dots connected by a line, it functions most effectively when you have greater than ten data points (categories). Your categories, though, just as in the column/bar charts, must be distinct, and if numeric, they must be evenly spaced. This is because the default settings will evenly space the data points across the X axis even if the underlying numbers in your categories aren't, in which case your data will be improperly distorted. Most stock price graphs you see are line graphs because the goal is to show variations across a significant amount of time—for example, a ninety-day trend of MSFT would have roughly sixty to sixty-five categories, and displaying these trends with a line is much easier on the eyeballs than sixty to sixty-five really skinny columns on a column chart.

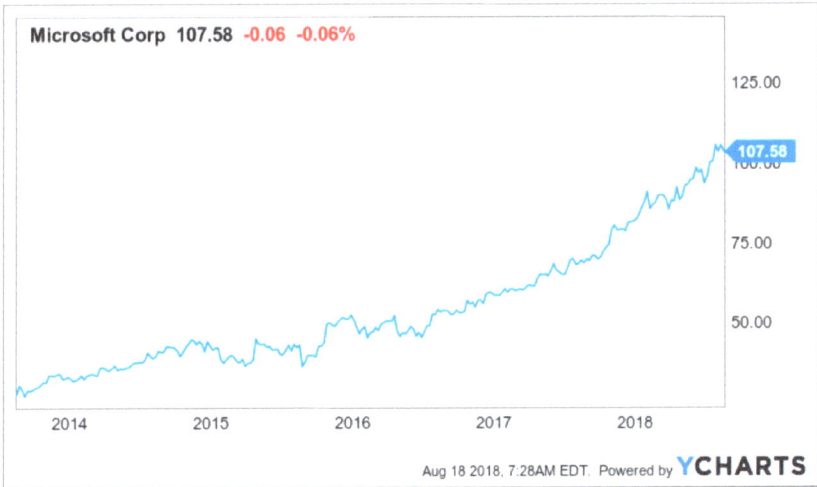

Microsoft Corp 107.58 -0.06 -0.06%

Aug 18 2018, 7:28AM EDT. Powered by YCHARTS

XY scatter plot: When you have a data set with one set of numbers and their corresponding coordinates, and you want to visualize the relationship between the two (or lack thereof), this is where the XY scatter plot comes into play. These generally work best when you have at least a handful of data points, and it works just as well with one hundred or more. An example would be a data set of babies born during a certain time period, plotting their birthweights against their body length at the time of birth to see what the correlation looks like. If you have a strong correlation between the sets of coordinates, it may make sense to have a line connecting the dots to improve the visual. If the data is more scattered (as the name implies), connecting them with a line will only confuse the display. Depending on your audience and what conclusions you want to reveal, adding a statistical trend line can be useful in showing a correlation to back up your claims.

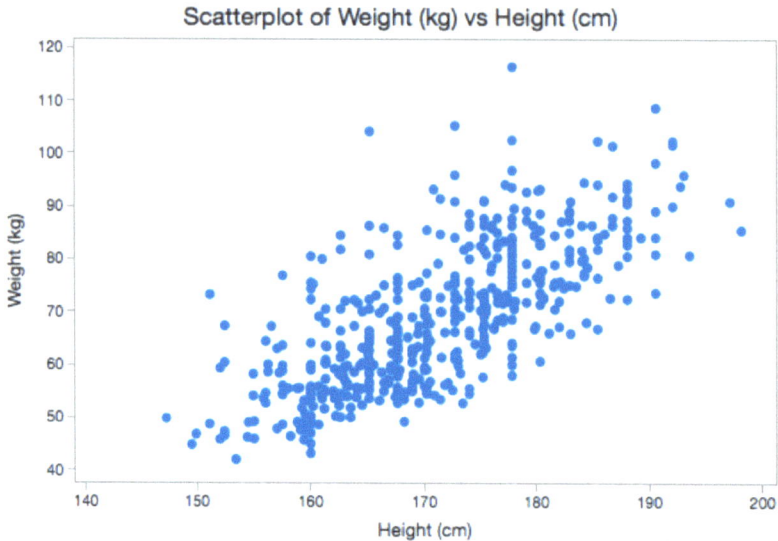

Scatterplot of Weight (kg) vs Height (cm)

Pie graph: Perhaps the most well-known in the graph format family is the pie graph. It is used to show the relative proportions of individual components that constitute the totality of the group. Examples would be the total population of South America broken out by country or the exit survey results among departing employees broken out by reasons for leaving the company. Each pie piece is sized based on its proportion to the entire group. In my South American population example, the Brazil pie piece would be almost half of the circle (211 million Brazilians out of the continent's 428 million inhabitants) while Suriname would have a tiny sliver representing its populace of 560,000. Pie charts can get dense and busy if you have too many different categories (slices); sometimes it is best to group smaller categories that may have like attributes, or if not terribly relevant to your story, a simple "Other" category will suffice, provided the "Other" bucket isn't a significant portion of the total.

Population Breakout of Continental South America by Country

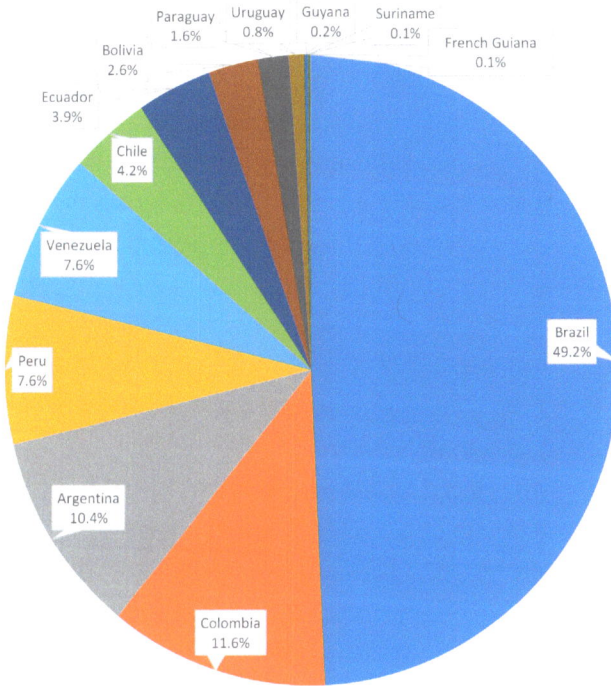

With the proper graph format chosen, you now need to get your data formatted appropriately inside the graph. The formatting tools can work with data organized in either rows or columns, but it doesn't always guess correctly. So if the thumbnail of the graph looks not at all like what you pictured in your head, it could be that the wizard thought you meant "rows" when you were hoping for "columns." Fortunately this is an easy fix. The exact location may vary by program, but in every program I have used there is a button that allows you to switch your data set from being read as "rows" to being read as "columns" and vice versa. Another common wizard failure is the occasional inclusion or exclusion of a "header row" or "header column." The header field is the label that you use to describe the category; in my South American example, these would be "country" and "population." The wizard may think that these are actually the first value in the series, and you will see a weird-looking data point on your chart or graph with these names (I didn't know there was a country called *Country*!). Alternatively, if you did not label your columns of data, the wizard may steal your first row to use it as the labels for each series, so instead of "country" it assumes your group of countries is labeled "Argentina." The bottom line message here is that while the graph formatters are pretty good at determining your intentions, they aren't perfect, and so be sure to inspect the resultant output to ensure that it makes logical sense.

Now that the data aspect of your chart or graph is in good shape, you need to adjust the other formatting levers to allow it to be as easily seen and understood as possible. During your presentation, it is generally considered a best practice to orient your audience to the data you are displaying by describing what each axis represents in your line graph, the population definition used in your pie graph, etc. You should, however, do your best formatting work so that the visual can stand on its own without requiring your verbal explanation. Several aspects of doing this are:

1. Make sure your chart or graph has a descriptive title (e.g., Population of South America by Country) and that your axes have similarly descriptive labels (e.g., birthweight in ounces).
2. Ensure that you have a legend if it is not clear what your data points represent. Generally speaking, for any column/bar chart, line graph, or XY scatter plot with more than one series, a legend is needed to show which series is which.
3. If you are using a bar/column chart, line graph, or XY scatter plot, it is likely that there will be gridlines added in both the horizontal and vertical directions. In my experience, it is often best to make these more muted than their default formatting or to outright eliminate them since they can detract from the core data.

4. Last, across all numbers and text, adjust the font size so that it is readable by your audience and highlights the right aspects. Your title should have the largest font size, and the legend text, axis labels, category labels, etc. should all be of similar size and sufficiently large. I have found that the default sizes in Microsoft Excel and PowerPoint are on the small side and often need to be jacked up a bit for proper readability.

Animate Responsibly

Have you ever sat through a presentation where the creator went overboard with busy and unnecessary animation from one slide to the next? If you have somehow been spared this travesty, you're one of the lucky ones. I have unfortunately had to endure many such episodes with fluttering diamonds and loud noises marking the transition of one slide to another, and others where objects take the slowest and most circuitous path to their resting destination on the screen.

Animation is a popular feature in PowerPoint and many other presentation programs, but in the business setting most of the bells and whistles in this toolbar should be left unclicked. That said, there is a time and a place for it, but if the sole purpose is to add showmanship to your deck, it's best to do without.

The most common use of animation that is business-appropriate is what I called the "staged reveal." This is when you have a set of bullets or objects on a single slide that, if needed to make your story come to life, should appear one at a time on the page instead of all at once when the slide is first presented. There are a variety of use cases, but the best animation feature to use is "appear," meaning the words or objects simply appear once you click the button or hit the space bar. No zooming in from left field, no pixie dust, and no bouncing. As for slide transitions, I generally advise that animation not be used since it creates more distraction than enhancement.

Sound and Video

There is certainly some allure when it comes to the use of multimedia features in your presentation. Many typical boring slideshows don't have them, so leveraging sound effects or video would help you stand out from the crowd and have your presentation reach higher levels of the memorability scale. Videos can be a great method for showcasing specific content that is otherwise very difficult to do. However, like any culinary use of spices, moderation and appropriateness are the key. Don't destroy an otherwise tasty pizza with too much oregano or ruin a cheesecake with cumin.

As mentioned in the animation section, sound effects are generally a bad idea if they do nothing more than accompany a slide transition or object animation. The audience can see the transitions occurring and don't need doorbells or wind chimes to ride shotgun with the slide change. There are cases where embedding an appropriate sound effect that is additive to your presentation can work well, but these cases are quite rare. So you shouldn't rule out the use of sound for eternity, but do not make it a regularly recurring cast member.

I last used sound effects in a presentation about eight years ago (to give you an idea of its infrequent use) during a presentation I was giving for a large audience where I had a quiz section that needed their participation. The format was such where I was seeking the top five answers to a particular survey question, and the conditions were right that I was able to have some fun with it. So I structured the slide and the associated animation as a *Family Feud* contest with the "Top Five Answers on the Board." As each correct answer was revealed, a sound was played that closely mirrored the "ding" sound heard on the popular TV game show. The audience got a kick out of this, and I received a lot of positive compliments afterward on the presentation, which I interpreted less as, "Wow those sound effects were really cool. How did you do that?" and more as, "Thank you for taking the extra time to make your presentation fun, interesting, and different from the seventeen others that were shown today."

Video is a bit of a different story. A well-produced, appropriate-length video can tremendously enhance your presentation if you can avoid these few common pitfalls:

Pitfall #1: The equipment in your presentation room doesn't support video. It could be that there are no speakers, bandwidth is too slow, or the projection quality is too weak. You might have the most amazing short video ever created in the history of modern business, but if your audience can't hear it or see it with a respectable resolution, it's dead on arrival.

Pitfall #2: You are unable to play the video on demand. I have personally witnessed live fumbling while the presenter tries to click a faulty link, switch to a different file, play a video from the cloud even though they are not connected to said cloud, and other embarrassing foibles. The message here is to thoroughly test your video in a true dress rehearsal (more on that in chapter 9) since you likely have fifteen to twenty seconds to get it playing before you lose your audience members to their smartphones to check email.

Pitfall #3: Your video is too long. Unless the video is the spotlight of your presentation, it needs to be no more than a few minutes long. The allocated time for an average presentation is somewhere in the range of thirty to forty-five minutes, so a video much longer than a few minutes will eat up a disproportionate amount of time for something that is simply an additive feature and not the focal point of the show.

Pitfall #4: Your video is too much window dressing and not enough content. It is unlikely that the success or failure of your presentation hinges upon your video production quality or ability, so if you are using this more as a show-off piece rather than supporting evidence of your recommendation, it would be better to edit down the pomp and circumstance or drop the idea altogether.

Copying and Pasting and Wasting

If your presentation is going to display some data, chances are that you are using a spreadsheet program such as Microsoft Excel to manage the information. Your spreadsheet program is going to have a lot more features for data display and graphing and charting, and you will find it tempting to copy and paste your data table or charts directly into your presentation. This action comes with a big yellow caution flag, and I will explain why.

While the option list looks much larger, there are essentially two ways that you can paste your table or graph into your presentation program: paste it as a picture or embed it in the file. Neither of these options are serious crimes, but if not handled properly, you can create problems with your presentation.

1. Paste as a picture: When you take this approach, your presentation program is taking a snapshot of the area selected in your spreadsheet, and it plops the snapshot into your slide or frame. From here forward, the only changes you can make to the picture are to adjust its size and its horizontal and vertical scale. As a rule, adjusting the horizontal and vertical scales independent of one another generally results in a distorted and at times terrible-looking graphic. If there are any words in your picture, they will either be shrunk together or stretched out as if you took them through the Funhouse of Mirrors at the carnival, and they didn't resume normalcy upon exiting. In other words,

if the default size of the picture in your presentation is not the exact size you would like, use only the corner adjustments so that it scales up or down in proportion to the original picture. If that doesn't work correctly, then you need to go back to your spreadsheet and adjust the scaling inside of that program in order to import something that can be scaled proportionally without distortion.

2. Embed the file directly: Sticking with the Microsoft suite as an example, if you copy a range of cells or a chart from Excel and paste it into PowerPoint, what is actually happening is that your spreadsheet file is being embedded in your PowerPoint file with your selected snapshot as the display. The good news is that you can make changes to the spreadsheet while inside the slide; the bad news is that your PowerPoint file has now taken on the weight of your Excel file, meaning that if you have a several MB spreadsheet, your presentation carries that heft in addition to the rest of its contents. This can create challenges in loading, saving, and sending the file if it is too large. To make matters potentially worse, if you make changes to the cell range inside of PowerPoint and the size of the Excel range changes, it may distort the ending display once you click out of it to return to the slide. This can be fixed, but it is often easiest to go back into Excel, make the changes, and then import the window all over again.

Both of these problems can be avoided if you use the table and chart functions inside of PowerPoint. They may not be as robust, but the data can easily be copied into a PowerPoint table or graph, and then any size adjustments made thereafter automatically preserve the proportion of the data and graphics without making your text look distractingly skinny or fat.

Run a Professionalism Scan

Once you have your presentation ready for prime time, take the time to read through it to ensure that you have a professional-looking product. On the content side, check for grammatical errors or confusing sentence structure within your text. Examine the layout for misalignments, object sizing or distortion issues, and consistency from one page or view to the next. Flip through the presentation to see how your transitions work and to make sure you have font consistency throughout. If you are concerned that you will miss something or do not have sufficient attention to detail, ask a friend or colleague to help you proofread it.

Chapter

8

ACCESSORIES

Congratulations on getting to this point. The bulk of the heavy lifting has been done, with a rock-solid narrative now bolstered with supporting data and commentary, all formatted in a highly attractive and professional file. The meat of the presentation is ready for consumption.

There are a few additional steps to be taken to fully accessorize your presentation—some that I would consider to be standard equipment while others are optional.

Standard Equipment

Title Page: This may go without saying, but your file should have a title page with a name of the presentation and the current date. Sounds simple, and it is, but your presentation would look naked without it.

Agenda: Rather than diving right into the background, it is generally helpful to insert a simple agenda page that steps through the four to six sections of your presentation. It is a useful visual for your audience to get a quick glance into how your presentation is organized, what you will be covering, and what the milestones are along the way so that they can mentally track progress. I have seen cases where the agenda page is copied and pasted to appear at each break point in the presentation. This tends to work best if you have very discrete pieces of your story or a very long story. This would be overkill for a brief five-slide update deck.

Optional Accessories

Executive Summary: This optional feature is essentially a one-page synopsis of your presentation, a CliffsNotes[2] version collapsed into a handful of bullets. Presumably this summary was popularized for the jet-setting executive who couldn't possibly sit through a thirty-minute presentation but can yea or nay your proposal while the town car shuttles her to a corporate jet bound for the Hamptons. An executive summary is usually only needed if directly requested or if you are sending your presentation to other important decision-makers who won't be attending your session. Ironically, you have already done most of the work to create this. An executive summary is essentially the same as your narrative. It may need to be shortened or have a few points omitted or consolidated, but the hard work is in your rearview mirror. The ideal executive summary is four to seven bullet-point sentences that cover the full range of your presentation from situation or background to recommendation and next steps.

Appendix: Just like the once-useful-but-no-longer-needed organ in your lower abdomen, the appendix of a presentation is sometimes there, sometimes not. It is used essentially as a reference section that may include additional information or data that was not needed to tell your core story but would come in handy for either a follow-up question or curious audience members who want to drill deeper. The appendix can be as long or as short as appropriate, and its contents do not need to be a part of the show unless called upon. As such, while appendix pages or frames shouldn't look like they were constructed by a first-grader, the effort to make them über-pretty like the slides of your main presentation is not worth it since they probably won't see the field.

---

[2] CliffsNotes is a registered trademark of Houghton Mifflin Harcourt.

Chapter **9**

DRESS REHEARSAL

You finally finished! You've created a compelling narrative, added all of your content into your presentation medium, and made sure that your work is aesthetically pleasing and error-free. Now all you have to do is to wait for your slot in the calendar to arrive, and then this effort will be in the books.

There is one more crucial step to take during this calm before the storm: a thorough dress rehearsal. Just because the presentation looks nice in print or electronic format doesn't mean that you'll wow your audience when it's go time.

There are a variety of ways you can prep for the big day, and you will need to prepare in whatever way works best for you personally. There are, however, a few different aspects of preparation that should be included in the rehearsal:

1. **Deliver the presentation to a fake audience.** This could be one or more work colleagues, your spouse or significant other, your pets, or an empty office. The point here is that you need to practice talking through the presentation to get a feel for what specific points you want to emphasize, what color commentary to include, what not to say, etc. This helps you avoid talking in circles, repeating statements, and reading exactly what is on your slide verbatim (pro tip: your audience can read what is

on your slide too). Practice also helps you to determine your uninterrupted pace of the presentation so you can adjust up or down the amount of time you are spending talking to account for the time allotted and for an appropriate reservation for questions from your audience.

2. **Make a list of potential questions or pushback you may receive.** While you may have the perfectly laid-out presentation, there will always be questions from your audience regardless of how obvious and straightforward your recommendations might be. Some people out there feel obligated to play devil's advocate and/or don't feel important unless they speak at least once during a meeting, so the questions will undoubtedly come. Due to time limits, your presentation won't answer all of them automatically, but anticipating the most likely questions that will surface and doing your homework to have thought through cogent responses will help you control the conversation and improve your chances of a successful outcome.

3. **Scout the venue where you will be presenting.** Many internal meetings are often booked with a specific conference room in advance. If this is the case, find a time when the conference is unoccupied (early morning or after hours are usually a good bet) and set up your presentation with the AV equipment just as you would do on game day. If you have a "road game"—a presentation outside of your company's offices such as at a client site, see if you can get access to the room early to set up and test the equipment. You will have a lot more time for preparation and adjustment in your own offices, but in either case you should ensure that the document projects properly for your audience, is scaled and focused correctly, and is large enough for your text to be readable in the back of the room. You can test audio features if you have sound or video in your presentation as well. This logistical aspect of your dress rehearsal will avoid the embarrassment of not being ready when your audience is ready.

In the planning process for your presentation, it is extremely important to budget time for the dress rehearsal. Don't put yourself in the position where you are finishing content and formatting in your presentation at the last minute, racing to the conference room with thumb drive in hand seconds before your show begins. Believe me, the absence of practice and logistical prep will be painfully obvious to your audience in one way or another.

10

ON THE FIELD ADJUSTMENTS: REACTING TO ROOM DYNAMICS DURING YOUR PRESENTATION

You planned. You designed. You dodged pitfalls. You reviewed. You practiced. You are so ready to deliver your presentation that you could do it in your sleep or standing on your head. You know what questions your audience will throw at you, and you have carefully crafted responses to each and every one. You arrive at the presentation venue, and someone tosses a wrench into your gear works:

"I know I told you that we had forty-five minutes for your presentation, but Cheryl is running late so we need to cut it to thirty."

"Rhonda, the SVP of Finance, is in town from corporate and wants to sit in on your presentation."

"Sorry, we had this room booked already. Chris didn't tell you? He said you guys were meeting in the Dungeon conference room downstairs instead."

"Shawn was supposed to be in the office today, but he's working from home because his beagle is sick, and he wants to do this via video."

Chances are you have at least observed some type of game-time change if you haven't actually experienced this with your own presentations. There is no need to pound the panic button; these wrinkles occur all the time and are easily solvable. Certainly if you are aware of the potential for a risk or two like this, you can add it to your dress rehearsal schedule of events.

Changes in Allotted Time

This may be the most frequent change you are likely to encounter, since many meetings often run long, unexpected issues pop up, and business priorities get clogged together and slow progress. It's just like the airlines: when the weather is perfect, passengers are all cooperative, nothing breaks down, and the airline workers all show up, so your flight will leave as scheduled. Mix in any degradation from this utopia and the five forty-five to LaGuardia doesn't even push back from the gate until almost seven. Such is the case with the delay in your afternoon presentation to the department VP.

If you have mastered your timing and pacing during dress rehearsal, compressing your presentation into a smaller time window should not be difficult. You know the important points that require emphasis or that are the critical elements of your story and those that still need room on the agenda in order to get your desired result. You still need a little time for questions, although the audience will understand that they may need to do more listening since a portion of your time has been pilfered. What you should not do is simply talk faster while following the exact same script.

In my experience, the places through which you can accelerate are the "situation" and "complication" in a recommendation or discussion story, and the "background" in an update story, since these are often understood at a high level being that they are the whole reason you started your project in the first place. As opposed to taking time to ensure that everyone has a full understanding of the foundational elements, they will need the abridged version here in order to ensure that you have the time to share your analysis, recommendations, important updates, and next steps while allowing at least a few minutes for questions.

In the rare case where you actually have more time than originally budgeted, you should proceed exactly as you practiced in your dress rehearsal. You will have more time for questions if needed, and if not, then you can shower your audience with the gift of time through an early ending to the meeting.

Changes in Audience

While not terribly common in my experience, the unplanned attendance of certain corporate or senior dignitaries is hard to predict and hard to plan for. Your best approach is to stick to your script since you have a well-planned story, and unless you are given any real notice, you don't have time to change your presentation anyway. If you can think on your feet, there may be situations where you can add a little bit of extra explanation on certain concepts if your new audience member isn't as familiar with the subject matter. You could also try to mix in any interesting notes or implications for them or the department they represent. In the fictional situation above, if Rhonda from Finance makes a cameo in your meeting, you can try to call out or more strongly emphasize any budgetary implications of your proposal as an example. On-the-fly catering to your audience is a nice plus if you can balance it while still maintaining the course you laid out. If you make no other enhancements during your presentation, the best advice is to not let the unexpected guest worry you and execute exactly as you rehearsed.

Changes in Venue

Depending on the layout and setup of your office, a conference room change may not be a big deal. Some companies are kind enough to their workers to have the same projectors, cabling, Wi-Fi network, etc. in all conference rooms, making your setup practice easily adaptable to the substitute room. Other companies are not so cooperative. Not that you need to conduct due diligence on every conference room in your office complex, which is a practical impossibility for a "road game" anyway, but if there are generally two or three rooms where the vast majority of the magic happens, it is worth familiarizing yourself with the equipment and networks for those rooms too, just in case you get bumped. Again, any homework you can do to avoid the discomfort of a lengthy launch of your presentation while your audience waits is time well spent.

Changes in Connection Method

One of the most common causes of technological fumbling to start a presentation is usually not the ability to display the file for the audience but is the act of connecting the full audience via audio or video channels. If you know up front that you will have remote audience members dialing in or connecting through videoconference, you would have already tested the systems from your side during your dress rehearsal. However, your audience base is not always as cooperative in ensuring that they can connect from their end in advance of the meeting. Despite what are perceived to be simple instructions, some people have trouble entering pass codes, adjusting camera settings, and downloading the latest version of Java or whatever else might be required to hear or see your presentation. Other times there are genuine issues with the audio or video host provider that can't be resolved instantaneously. Given this, I recommend having a foolproof backup plan that at least allows everyone to connect through audio so they can hear you present while following along with the materials with the file or link you sent them through email.

Occasionally, you will find a situation where you are asked to spin up an audio or video link on demand due an unexpectedly remote audience member. No need to panic; this is not your audience testing you and your ability to improvise. You will be afforded a little extra time to establish said connection to reunite your audience virtually. That said, you should have these cards up your sleeve—you can earn some valuable street cred if you can effortlessly make Shawn's unshaven mug appear on the screen next to your title page, a helpful skill to add to your repertoire during your preparation.

Once you start presenting, while it is important to execute as planned during your dress rehearsal, it is also important to read your audience as you speak so that you can make subtle adjustments to maintain their maximum engagement. Of course to do this, you need to not direct your speech toward the screen but rather make eye contact with the individuals around the room. This will help you look for cues on what tweaks you should make.

Pacing Cues

Just because the boss or client made the presentation request does not guarantee that he or she will be highly engaged during the live show. However, it is important that you make every effort to keep them engaged during your entire presentation despite the goldfish-like attention spans that they may possess. Inappropriate pacing is one of the leading causes of disinterest, and the majority of the time your plot is simply advancing too slowly.

How can that be? You practiced your delivery nine times in front of seven mock audiences (Rover and Mittens didn't mind seeing it twice) and you had your pacing down to a science. That may all be true, but how were you to know that your presentation was on the same day as Budget Tuesday, which has your VP's mind lingering elsewhere even though you really need a decision from her today.

Your VP may not directly tell you, but if she is frequently peeking at her phone, looking out the window, checking her watch, or doodling on your handouts, it's a good sign that her engagement needs resuscitating. If simple eye contact and the otherwise beautiful and compelling content of your presentation aren't providing sufficient rejuvenation, one tactic is to pick up the speed of your presentation to shorten the path to the punch line. Remember, this isn't about talking faster but focusing on more important points in order to turn pages or frames more quickly.

The Quiet Audience

Another tactic to use with a potentially disengaged audience is to pause and ask if there are any questions. To be even more direct, you can ask an individual member if he or she has any questions. This can work well if there is a specific stakeholder in the room or if you are getting the silent treatment from the key decision-maker. Either way, if your audience is really quiet, one of three things is likely happening:

1. Your presentation is so clear and to the point that you are preemptively answering any questions they could possibly conjure up.
2. Your presentation, despite your careful planning and preparation, has missed its mark so badly that your audience (a) doesn't know where to start or (b) is simply hoping for it to be over as soon as possible.
3. Despite the high-quality product you are displaying, your audience is so distracted by reasons beyond your control. This means that you may be getting an easy rubber stamp to your recommendation, but if not, then you need to follow up with

your boss for a WTF conversation on why you put so much work into something that no one seems to care about.

The Chatty Audience

In my experience, the more common audience flavor is the question-happy variety since most people either like to hear themselves talk or have been given an informal quota of two questions per meeting regardless of their relative import. In these situations, instead of pulling teeth from a reticent group, you are now trying to graciously address three times more questions than what you planned for during your dry runs.

There is a natural temptation to answer every question that comes your way on the spot, regardless of sequence and whether or not it fits the flow of your story. Don't feel overly compelled to do so: if you are still on page three of your presentation and someone asks a question that will be answered automatically on page six, simply respond that you will answer that exact question in a couple of slides. It is okay to do this for two reasons: (1) it is a very short reply that takes just a few seconds, and (2) it allows you to preserve the flow of your narrative without getting out of sequence.

There may be situations, however, where due to a compressed time slot or an up-front barrage of questions that a "skip ahead" question could be a great way to accelerate your presentation. Instead of postponing that aspect of the discussion, you could instead offer to jump to that page of the deck to adjust directly to the clearly stated interest of the audience.

No matter how you handle it, the reality with chatty audiences is that you have less time to deliver your content without being completely disrespectful. So deploying the same tactics as the compressed time allotment situation will help you get through the necessary components of your material while giving the audience what it needs.

You may find yourself in a situation where there are so many questions that the chances of you actually completing your update or securing feedback on your recommendation are as good as hitting green on the roulette wheel. In these cases, there are three different paths you can choose:

1. Bravely but politely ask if people could hold their questions until the end in order to finish your story and get everyone out of the meeting on schedule.
2. Ask if the group can stay longer in order to complete the discussion.
3. Schedule a session at a later time to finish the conversation.

You will need to read your audience here to make the right call, but to somewhat state the obvious, don't settle for option #3 if you need direction or a decision urgently.

Chapter **11**

FEEDBACK AND A DEEP BREATH

Whew! You survived your assignment and live to fight another day in the corporate war. And you are now much better prepared for your next presentation battle when the request comes in. Take a deep breath and give yourself a much-deserved pat on the back.

In many cases, as you should now be able to see, there are follow-up activities to be done. Perhaps you received some questions that you couldn't answer on the spot, and more data or research is needed. Maybe your recommendation was actually approved, and now you need to put the wheels in motion on the next step of your project. Or you advanced to step five in a nine-step sales process with your client, and you need to strategize on how to get past step six. In any of these cases, you should have picked up some feedback from your audience on what needs to happen next; what you may not have received is any feedback on how your presentation could have been better.

This brings us to the final stage of your journey: soliciting feedback on your effort. If your audience wasn't openly forthcoming on what would have turned your show from an A- to an A+, you should ask them. This can be done in whatever format you find most comfortable, but a simple follow-up email to the audience members to thank them for their time and to see if they have any feedback for you is an easy activity that can pay significant dividends in the future. Each person has his own way of processing information, and this detail is not generally tattooed on his arm in bold print, so if you don't ask, you may never find out.

Don't expect responses from everyone—in fact, you may get responses from no one. However, any feedback received, even if a mere confirmation of your stellar performance is all you get, is still valuable in ensuring your next presentation is as good as or better than the one you just completed. Such is the circle of professional development in the corporate world.

We have arrived at the close. I hope you found this valuable and at least a smidge entertaining. If you have any feedback, feel free to email me at mason@masonargiropoulos.com. This chapter would feel hypocritical if I wasn't open to feedback myself.

In the meantime, take another deep breath; heck, even take a day off Ferris-Bueller-style. Just make sure your time off request is approved by your manager.

www.ingramcontent.com/pod-product-compliance
Lightning Source LLC
Chambersburg PA
CBHW041711200326
41518CB00001B/155